Scales & Arpeggios for Piano

J Koh's Fingering Method   Grade 4

How To Use The Book

B major

R.H.	1	2♯	3♯	1	2♯	3♯	4♯	1	2♯	3♯	1	2♯	3♯	4♯	[5]
L.H.	4	3♯	2♯	1	4♯	3♯	2♯	1	3♯	2♯	1	4♯	3♯	2♯	[1]

Place the both hands on the key note B. Play the B major scale ascending, 2 octaves, according to the fingering indicated above. This scale requires five sharps, thus the fingering 2♯ 3♯ 4♯. The highest note at the top of the scale is indicated with a box [5]. Now play the scale descending, this time moving backwards. You will be surprised how quickly you learn your scales!

This method employs visual recognition of numerals with tactile co-ordination to assist the learning of scales and arpeggios. When playing hands together, **gaps** in the method refer to *turns led by the right hand*. Fingering of the left hand is placed in line with that of the right hand to ensure good co-ordination. Sharps are indicated on the right side of the fingering to show a raised note while flats are placed on the left for lowered notes. Effective rhythmic grouping is shown by notation on the staves.

Teachers and students are <u>not</u> obliged to follow the fingering patterns. Alternative fingering is occasionally provided in brackets. The size of hands and length of fingers vary and thus other alternatives are possible as long as a good legato touch, evenness of tone and smoothness of execution are achieved. Try to keep fingers curved and listen carefully to the sound produced. Metronome speeds are suggested for practice and examination purposes.

Josephine Koh

Published by
Wells Music Publishers
896 Dunearn Road
Sime Darby Centre #04-03
Singapore 589472

Copyright 2008 © by Wells Music Publishers
ISBN 978-981-08-1295-9

All rights reserved. This book or part thereof may not
be reproduced in any form or by any means, electronic or
mechanical, including photocopying, recording or any information
storage and retrieval system now known or to be invented without
prior permission from the publisher.

Cover design by Lee Kowling

Typesetting by Yvonne Choo and Mifiona Quah

Edited by David Saw

Scales & Arpeggios for Piano

GRADE 4

Major Scales of B, B♭, E♭, A♭ and D♭

Minor Scales of C♯, G♯, C and F

Contrary Motion Scales of F and E♭ majors; D and C minors

Chromatic Scales on BLACK keys

Arpeggios of B, B♭, E♭, A♭ and D♭ majors; C♯, G♯, C and F minors

Major Scales

Hands separately and together in similar motion: 2 octaves

Starter's speed ♩ = 92   Minimum exam speed ♩ = 52   Recommended speed ♩ = 60

HS + HT

✓ **B major**   B + E   NATURALS

| R.H. | 1 | 2♯ | 3♯ | 1 | 2♯ | 3♯ | 4♯ | 1 | 2♯ | 3♯ | 1 | 2♯ | 3♯ | 4♯ | [5] |
| L.H. | 4 | 3♯ | 2♯ | 1 | 4♯ | 3♯ | 2♯ | 1 | 3♯ | 2♯ | 1 | 4♯ | 3♯ | 2♯ | [1] |

✓ **B♭ major**   HS + HT   C + F NATURAL

| R.H. | ♭2 | 1 | 2 | ♭3 | 1 | 2 | 3 | ♭4 | 1 | 2 | ♭3 | 1 | 2 | 3 | [♭4] |
| L.H. | ♭3 | 2 | 1 | ♭4 | 3 | 2 | 1 | ♭3 | 2 | 1 | ♭4 | 3 | 2 | 1 | [♭2] |

✓ **E♭ major**   HS + HT

| R.H. | ♭2 | 1 | 2 | ♭3 | ♭4 | 1 | 2 | ♭3 | 1 | 2 | ♭3 | ♭4 | 1 | 2 | [♭3] |
| L.H. | ♭3 | 2 | 1 | ♭4 | ♭3 | 2 | 1 | ♭3 | 2 | 1 | ♭4 | ♭3 | 2 | 1 | [♭2] |

Minor Scales

Hands separately and together in similar motion: 2 octaves
Candidates can choose either melodic or harmonic

Starter's speed ♩ = 92   Minimum exam speed ♩ = 52   Recommended speed ♩ = 60

C♯ melodic minor

OR

C♯ harmonic minor

G♯ melodic minor (enharmonic A♭)

OR

G♯ harmonic minor (enharmonic A♭)

TIPS: As you go up look for semitones
Look for E – G

C melodic minor

| R.H. | 1 2 ♭3 | 1 2 3 4 | 1 2 ♭3 | 1 2 3 4 |5| |
| L.H. | 5 4 ♭3 | 2 1 3 2 | 1 4 ♭3 | 2 1 3 2 |1| |

| ♭4 ♭3 2 1 | ♭3 2 1 | ♭4 ♭3 2 1 | ♭3 2 1 |
| ♭2 ♭3 1 2 | ♭3 4 1 | ♭2 ♭3 1 2 | ♭3 4 5 |

OR

C harmonic minor ✓

3s always together on flats

| R.H. | 1 2 ♭3 | 1 2 ♭3 4 | 1 2 ♭3 | 1 2 ♭3 4 |5| |
| L.H. | 5 4 ♭3 | 2 1 ♭3 2 | 1 4 ♭3 | 2 1 ♭3 2 |1| |

7

F melodic minor

R.H.	1 2 ♭3 ♭4	1 2 3	1 2 ♭3 ♭4	1 2 3 [4]
L.H.	5 4 ♭3 ♭2	1 3 2	1 4 ♭3 ♭2	1 3 2 [1]

♭3 ♭2 1	♭4 ♭3 2 1	♭3 ♭2 1	♭4 ♭3 2 1
♭2 ♭3 1	♭2 ♭3 4 1	♭2 ♭3 1	♭2 ♭3 4 5

OR

Practise more
#7
E

F harmonic minor

R.H.	1 2 (♭3)(♭4)	1 (♭2) 3	1 2 ♭3 ♭4	1 (♭2) 3 [4]
L.H.	5 4 ♭3 ♭2	1 ♭3 2	1 4 ♭3 ♭2	1 ♭3 2 [1]

Contrary Motion Scales
Major and Harmonic Minor Scales
Hands together, beginning and ending on key note: 2 octaves

Starter's speed ♩ = 92   Minimum exam speed ♩ = 52   Recommended speed ♩ = 60

F major   *thumbs Fs and Cs coming back. 4Bb 3E*

| R.H. | 1 2 3 ♭4 | 1 2 3 | 1 2 3 ♭4 | 1 2 3 [4] |
| L.H. | 1 2 3 1 | ♭2 3 4 | 1 2 3 1 | ♭2 3 4 [5] |

E♭ major

| R.H. | ♭2 1 2 ♭3 ♭4 | 1 2 ♭3 | 1 2 ♭3 ♭4 | 1 2 [♭3] |
| L.H. | ♭2 1 2 ♭3 ♭4 | 1 2 ♭3 | 1 2 ♭3 ♭4 | 1 2 [♭3] |

D harmonic minor

| R.H. | 1 2 3 | 1 2 (♭3 4♯) | 1 2 3 | 1 2 ♭3 4♯ [5] |
| L.H. | 1 2♯ ♭3 | 1 2 3 4 | 1 2♯ ♭3 | 1 2 3 4 [5] |

look out for Ab and Eb
Do more practise

C harmonic minor Eb

R.H.	1	2	♭3	1	2	♭3	4	1	2	♭3	1	2	♭3	4	5
L.H.	1	2	♭3	1	2	♭3	4	1	2	♭3	1	2	♭3	4	5

Ab

Chromatic Scales

Hands separately and together: 2 octaves

Starter's speed ♩ = 108   Minimum exam speed ♩ = 52   Recommended speed ♩ = 66

Beginning on any BLACK key:

$$D^♭, E^♭, G^♭, A^♭, B^♭$$

OR

$$C^♯, D^♯, F^♯, G^♯, A^♯$$

Play each black key with ♭**3**. Use **1 2** on adjacent white keys.

Example:

Beginning on A♭ (Only 1 octave is shown)

R.H.	♭3	1	♭3	1	2	♭3	1	♭3	1	2	♭3	1	♭3
L.H.	♭3	1	♭3	2	1	♭3	1	♭3	2	1	♭3	1	♭3

Arpeggios
Hands separately and together in root position: 2 octaves
Starter's speed ♩ = 56   Minimum exam speed ♩ = 76   Recommended speed ♩ = 80

HS + HT

B major

B♭ major   HS + HT

11

HS + HT

Common Fingering for E♭ major, A♭ major and D♭ major

R.H.　　♭2　1　♭2　♭4　1　♭2　|♭4|

L.H.　　♭2　1　♭4　♭2　1　♭4　|♭2|
　　　　(♭3)　　　　　　　　　　(♭3)

E♭ major

A♭ major

D♭ major (enharmonic C♯)

Common Fingering for C♯ minor and G♯ minor

C♯ minor

G♯ minor (enharmonic A♭)

Common Fingering for C minor and F minor

R.H.	1	♭2	3	1	♭2	3	5
L.H.	5	♭3 (♭4)	2	1	♭3 (♭4)	2	1

C minor

F minor

END

Best-Selling Titles

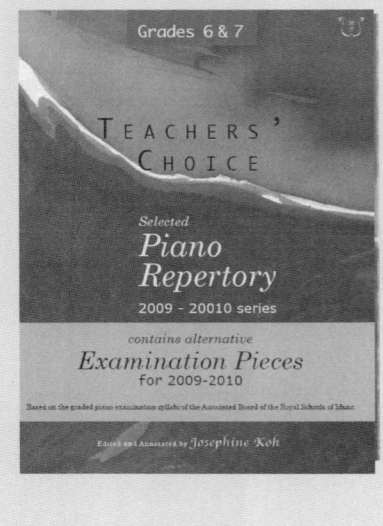

Teachers' Choice, Selected Piano Repertory Examination Pieces for 2009-2010 Series
Edited and Annotated by Josephine Koh

A refreshing new publication which comprises popular and alternative works from the ABRSM Piano Examination syllabus. These pieces are specially selected to provide students with a comprehensive and varied repertoire. Meticulously fingered and edited, *Teachers' Choice* offers teachers and students alike added performance and teaching directions. Scores in *Teachers' Choice* are beautifully set and annotated for excellent reading.

Available from Grades 1 to 8.

Practice in Music Theory
Revised Edition
by Josephine Koh

The revised edition of the *Practice in Music Theory* series is a set of highly recommended instructional workbooks for students who wish obtain a sound foundation in music theory. The *J Koh's* teaching approach is academic and logical, yet musically conceived. Progressive topics are set out to guide students through their understanding of the fundamental musical concepts and ideas. Based on the requirements of the ABRSM theory syllabus, this Grade 2 book contains:

- clear teaching points and graphical illustrations
- explanatory notes that are consistently applied throughout the series
- exercises of progressive difficulty that provide students with sufficient practice to master the topics and concepts learnt
- updated information and study notes that are most effective for reference and revision.

Available from Grades 1 to 8.

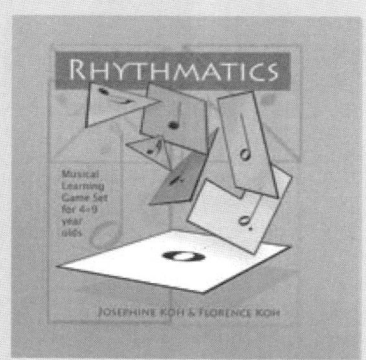

Rhythmatics
by Josephine Koh

Group notes, write beats, identify time signatures and complete bars with missing notes or rests — all these tasks with Rhythmatics, the most sought after musical learning aid for young children. Attractive colour cards, each with a particular colour and shape corresponds to a specific time value. With the cards to be arranged on the base whiteboard mathematically, the child visualises the concept instantaneously and is able to perceive the number of beats in a bar. Most suitable for children between ages of 4 to 9, Rhythmatics is recommended for the study of music theory up to Grade 2.